I0519324

A RECORD
OF CHANGE

THADDEUS DUGAN

A RECORD OF CHANGE

by Thaddeus Dugan

Anamcara Press LLC

Published in 2024 by Anamcara Press LLC
Author © 2024 Thaddeus A. Dugan
Book design by Maureen Carroll
Georgia, Timeburner, and Minion Pro.
Printed in the United States of America.

Book Description: Dugan's debut collection explores the evolution of the soul when age can no longer be used as an excuse not to change or when the pain becomes too great to remain the same. These poems reflect the rigorous self-examination it takes to reinvent yourself. Through love, grief, and loss The author does this, while never losing sight of his collective humanness.

ANAMCARA PRESS LLC
P.O. Box 442072, Lawrence, KS 66044
https://anamcara-press.com/

Ordering Information:
Quantity sales. Special discounts are available on quantity purchases by corporations, associations, and others. For details, contact the publisher at the address above.
Orders by U.S. trade bookstores and wholesalers. Please contact Ingram Distribution.

Dugan, Thaddeus, Author
A Record of Change
POE023020 POETRY / Subjects & Themes / Love & Erotica
POE023070 POETRY / Subjects & Themes / War *
POE023010 POETRY / Subjects & Themes / Death, Grief, Loss
POE023050 POETRY / Subjects & Themes / Family

ISBN-13: 978-1-960462-36-7 (Paperback)
ISBN-13:978-1-960462-37-4 (Hardcover)

Library of Congress Control Number: 2023951568

Some of us aspire to the stars even though it is much safer on the ground.

Contents

DEDICATION—

To the Dugan & Cameron Clans

PART I: Becoming

Plans

Deep in a cavern
chaos craves sound.
This restlessness resides
in a persistence so loud
it is unheard of,
with plans to take the world by storm.

But champions aren't born
they are made.
In a kiln
under the supervision of fire.
Mind the kiln-sitter
& the hands of clay will transform.

Some Context for You Early Morning Listeners

A little context so you can feel
the rough edges of my existence
and through some rigid shadow work
my imbued darkness now
collaborates with the stars
which always align in hindsight.

I remember the distant faces
and the rooms where perfume
would black out the sun,
then I'd neglect a few years
by being in love
and in that destruction
being dumb,
some would say reckless.
There is no such thing
when you are cold and numb,
in the confined spaces of youth.
We are briefly beautiful
but cannot conceptualize
convinced by a preposterous mirror
that reads our mind
then tells us back our own lies.
The uncomfortable skin,
where I'd hide in a bath
and change the mask,
peel it off then plaster on
a subsequent grin.
Putting the former to the side,
just in case,

in hopes that I might find
one to wear for eternity.
One that would let me
bat all the eyes,
one that could help me
do better than just get by.

Once I understood
that my version of me
was a creation of my own mind,
I whittled my actions into purpose
gave them something to earn,
to yearn for,
like a portion of the sky.
And I'm happy with the skin
that was given to me,
stretching out over the density
of cheek bones, to form
the smile you see today.
These poems are a record of my change.

These days you can pick apart my life
all you'll do is pick apart the scars,
for shadow work declutters the space
leaves a place, a pause for me to follow my heart,
and that warmth leads me,
wherever I need to go.
Instead of relying on that harshest of critics
The sly voice my ego.

A Means to an End

It's a gloomy Friday and busy,
traffic on display.
The disarray of people
traversing the halls,
if I'm not careful, I'll take home
remnants of a bad day.
In the ER they tell me to come,
do a deceased clean, and I ask,
"What's the difference
between cleaning for the vacant
or the breathing?"
It just seems dirtier
with apprehension marooned
in an empty room,
leaving a film over all I do
this day.

The dream is a vision,
a mere want-to-be
circling the trees above.
Blurry
from the maze of days
out of the spectrum.
It'll come into eyesight
further in life,
and from underneath I wait
as the breeze cripples the haze
of aspirations buried
in a cavern so deep.
I can hear them resonating
can't quite make out

what's being said
as I clean the toilet seat.

There's this residue that exists
beyond any known premise,
perhaps
I was never quite sane to begin with.
Nor am I now in chasing them
listing to one side,
listless on the inside,
maybe I should have been safe,
been a doctor, been a lawyer.
In an aha moment I hear,
"It's no better to be safe than sorry and ..."

If this coil should ascend
will it look down
and covet the distress,
of what could have
or could have not been?
Serving as a potent reminder,
if everything was such a cinch,
what God would we call on,
if any?

I cursed the tide
the first time
it came in,
for little did I know
it wouldn't drown me
and would recede. So,
I'll test the waters again.

The World has Lost its Color

Days flash in the mirror.
The same day there
disappears,
somehow into the now.

An imposing dark mass
accumulates in the west.
Droplets thud next to my footsteps,
leave dimples in the dirt.

Breeze breaks into wind,
the sopping violence
slaps against my skin
until the silence... Drips
on occasion.

A rain gauge brims
from the passing storm
and so it warns of the peril
from further downpours
if I continue to neglect the excess.

I dump the contents,
and as the minutes
fill in with emptiness.
I can't stand that even more.

No Closer to Home

I met with a friend
the other day
who'd been lost in the swell
of material things.
Since
he was completely convinced
that he could travel the world,
navigate the barriers of language,
and find spirituality.
Somewhere outside of himself,
I frowned under my breath
as he left to scale mount Everest.
A few months later he called
from Tibet with an updated forecast,
"There I was on the crest,
below the clouds, stood long and lone
a stone's throw from heaven.
No sign of man, no sign of God.
There I found myself alone
only the snow bitten wind in my hair,
with nothing outside myself to know,
and just like everywhere else on earth,
I was no closer to home."

A Southwest Vacay

They keep the rough patches hidden real well in the city,
behind the gleam of outlet malls,
away from the veneer finish of the suburbs.
And dawn strikes me
as uncharacteristically somber,
for the mess is no longer
a product of the dark.

I tell my girlfriend,
"I'll trade you in for a newer model,
one that's got the crazy cornered
or a bottle, what's the difference?"
On the tenth day in it's been a long trip,
as I try & pull it back together.
The stitches begin to stretch
start to rip, so I walk
out on the edge of decadence,
where I am reintroduced to the fear of God.

A mob of cops pull into a parking lot
skidding to a stop.
A deluge of drug dealers disperse
from the rail of a Motel 6 mezzanine
by any means possible,
like roaches running from the light.
And junkies,
(who feed at these flophouses)
unpack their belongings from shopping carts
at 8:15 in the morning,
all along the sidewalk.
Living in the symptom,

that a fix will help them
recover from their doldrums,
or just hoping to die in the meantime.

I breathe in the dread.
I wanted to belong; isn't that what we all lack?
But this skin has a smear of sadness that prohibits any-
one from looking in,
until the solution slowly dwindles down the throat and
alters my condition to fit
and at any consequence.
As I rub the context of these words on my neck.
Nowadays, I'll tell you how mistaken enough we are to be
exquisite,
and when all is said and done we shun ourselves the
most.
If all I do is stay clean for the rest of this tour it'll be
amazing
but that's not what staying clean is for.

What have We Got to Lose

Wind assails the tallgrass,
undulates the blades
flat into the face of a nation
as an armada of hands wave at a barricade.
Ground control sounds T-minus ten,
the picture dips
as attention rips back to the landing pad.
Propulsion begins and the ship lifts
into the distance until it disappears
to the cheers of a rambunctious crowd.

On the monitor, I see farewells.
My grip tightens around the G's I feel,
I am the imposter in this seat.
As I retreat back into this body
the ship shatters the atmosphere
and the stars descend upon me
like sprinkles in the first sense of spring,
when I know I am done enduring.

Looking at the clouds
slowly moving by, from above.
I wonder if anyone is seeing
the same scene from below
and enjoying it as much as I
in free fall?

Light shimmers off steel waves
like white phosphorous
as the fuchsia of a late sun sets in
on my distaste.
Clouds dissipate into wispy shavings,
holes peek through the dense night.
As stars sneak into a hemispheric-view
where time and space together
beat against the shore of my ruin.

I see the space station race by,
cascading the outskirts of earth
like a meteorite in a shallow arc.
And wonder why I didn't pursue
what I always dreamed of.
The next day I cut
the safety net of a cush job,
and write like my life depends on it.
For what have we got to lose?

All Equal

I watch the echocardiogram
beat repeatedly in an off-beat,
the rhythm of my heart.
I can hear it
start to flutter,
a warm pumping
inside my ears,
pulsating in the fear
of what's not being said
about the outcome as
they make me wait.
Like I have the patience
to keep investing
in a future that
may not be intact.
I sit and soak in silence
to counteract the disturbance.
But here I am and there it is
wherever I go.

I've imagined my demise a few times,
a group of unscripted shorts
running the course,
traveling the segments
of a lifetime where
we divine our own lies.
We hide behind mild success,
behind some words,
until they obsess into vapor,
for we are all equals,
held captive by the absence of breath.

And this is where we do our best
to make peace with ourselves
before we die.
So there's no need to rush
towards the end.
When the body begins to outlast its purpose,
and we've surplus hours
to consider the grim.
Placate the past,
make it as fast as you can.
We spend the first half learning bad habits
and the last half learning to live without them.

Progression

Metamorphosis consists of
a slow draw of articulate findings,
trailing a pen that keeps writing
well after stale beliefs begin to deteriorate.
We pluck and pull through the fabric of our trials,
in the midst of our own devices,
in search for perfection.
No mention of voids.
Here come the junctures, the needlepoint pricks and
punctures.
Only in the depth of reflection do we become aware,
the focal point minced in deception
until the sutures heal, at least enough to backfill.
Somewhere along the venture
we accumulate a faith in self,
re-sculpt a persona, relying on strengths.
We distribute the wealth to multiple aspects,
dissecting our beliefs in hopes for more,
not limited by anyone's interpretation,
not cemented anywhere anyone wants us to be.
Get some distance between the date
where fate decided to change you drastically.
Find a niche and etch your name all over a generation,
comprised of a few renowned works here and there.

Crisp and Renewed

I take a walk in the woods,
they're downtrodden.
Fingery sticks will soon bud with crowded cliques,
as the excerpts of snow begin to go.
I barely make it out with my wits intact.
The path curls under a bridge
where shade collects in a separate coolness
over the shale bottom of a see-through creek.
Pillars project across the top of water,
a goose honks, it reverberates in wavelengths.
Bobbing along the surface,
his trail ripples the standing pillars.
The stream comes upon a shallow rapid,
water makes its way around the edge,
the depth keeps the rocks at bay.
This is where I come to contemplate.
Night is approaching as I enter a clearing
with a 360-degree view,
far enough that the glare from the city
doesn't dim the starlight.
The piercing spring sky has me crisp and renewed.

Hindsight is an Optical Illusion

Dark inklings,
reeking from my tongue,
sinking into,
the vibration of a still eardrum,
preparing me,
for the worst of the worst outcomes.
A stranger stands by a house that
I drive by to reconcile,
with the people inside,
who once lived there,
who I used to know,
who overdosed.
Some days I forget about them,
they creep back into my repeating,
my nose won't quit bleeding,
from baby-step falls,
banging my head,
using indentations as footholds,
to scale the same sorry walls.
18 months in the distillation,
of a diluted evaluation process.
Hindsight is an optical illusion,
for without the experience where would I be?
Without the confusion,
how could I see past the bloody noses?
One door opens, then another closes,
gluing together the pieces of esteem,
in the resurrection of what once was a dream,

when everything comes together
in that exact moment when it needs to.
I'll exceed everything I was ever expected to be
by just being me.

Pipe Dreams

They come and go, you know,
in for a few then gone,
back to getting trampled on by the streets.

As we speak,
I'm taking up a dead man's seat.
That's what happens when you're loaded in a pipe dream.

I'm intolerant tonight, anything anybody says
I roll my eyes at a self-help group,
the anonymous kind.
I know his nomenclature before he states it,
an addict, methamphetamine, you can tell by his shifty
means,
prison tatts and an extract of his time down,
tube socks pulled up to his knees add to his street cred.
Next,
there's an intermediary between heaven and earth,
Jesus will save you if you throw in your lot,
getting on peoples nerves,
these preachers never seem to last beyond a few tasks of
self-examination.
Then the heroin addict,
pasty-faced in withdrawals,
usually hangs out in the bathroom stalls,
stabbing at holes in a self-induced coma,
living for the aroma of vinegar.

My first inclination is to point out our discrepancies,
like I'm some type of better.
We all share the desire to quit;
this is where I come to sit in between fits of insanity.
When addiction taps at the bedroom window,
half-heard through bamboo sheets,
prying into sleep.
Before I relapse into
drones overhead humming behind blinds,
in the absence of sun where secrets hide.
I tell myself when it's done,
I'll look back at the aftermath of a derecho
which has passed,
leaving regret stapled together with lies.
Now I'm trying something different.

So I need these people to show me how to act right,
and sometimes just to sit tight to keep the voices,
from echoing into a faction, a coup, then entering into
action.
And in this uncertainty, I wonder
who will I end up being?
What will I need to fail at to become me?
If I fail too miserably who'll take my seat?

Reflections on the Discord

In its entirety
you know it's all futile right?
The musical chairs we play with lovers.
The curses we spit above.
The long awkward glances at mishaps,
knowing better but having had to endure.
The success we hoped to invest,
in having positive impact on others.

Though in those vast moments
it was all worthwhile.

The closed-eyed kisses that ended with a grin,
even when things went amiss.
The mistakes that raked us over coals,
that taught us what and what was not blissful.
The people who helped us forgive,
cause we did it for ourselves, not them.

And in the vacancies,
countenance juxtaposed,
acting indifferent when wanting that someone to notice.
Jumbled in the diversity
of searching for more than a pretext in discord.
In a misconstrued version
something will make us full again,
instead of looking in at an exact replica
and accepting the reflection.

In the Current

I hear the quiver
when the river refuses to stand still.
The quiver of daffodils,
as the lilies hang their heads in prayer.

PART II: Those Who Taught Me to Let Go

Home

Give me warmth
then leave me be
for the only thing I know for certain,
is if you get too close
then I will be finished
when you leave.

I'll tell you how frail the human heart is,
how it hums from first love,
how it fails to fully mend,
then pushes everyone else away
who attempts to stay there-after.

How I knew a girl who could do no wrong,
with a tiny cannister of blood
hung about her neck
and not one speck of grief
for the promise she wouldn't keep.

How her beauty had me
on uneven ground, in a pasture
in the next town,
our indentions smeared in the wheat,
on the outskirts of a timid belief
that I may find a home.
Home: a place where I can stow
tiny bits of myself,
so that they may grow safe
from the ever-eclipsing hate
of this world.
How she left me cold.

In the sweltering heat of that summer,
how she taught me to house my own home,
to dig deep into my soul,
make it my stomping grounds
to build a foundation to bear
whatever the future could hold.

Rubble

In the throes of morning,
before the strain
of inventing my own worries,
like snow flurries in summer.
Silently choreographed to fit no needs,
only to fuel unpleasantries.
And once the precipice has been reached
It's time again to lay siege
to the rubble.

Staring into a separate space,
the lines on my face have been erased by youth.
I fall victim to the game,
save everyone in the room,
jump on a hand grenade,
take one for the team.
She'll spit me out soon
like a Venus flytrap.
And who's next is a craps shoot.

Now I'm a pool of emptiness,
like the choices I choose,
like the shoes of my father,
like lost souls who contribute to this muse,
popping off the top of a bottle
that has already been consumed,
to dilute the senses yesterday
in a lifelong chase to get away.

Since Removed

As symbolic as the frolicking tumble of fallen leaves,
your presence is a pristine image preoccupying that mys-
tery
where we would sit and coalesce with the breeze.
Our noses upturned to savor the cool sound of shaking
trees.
I was drawn to you like a shadow to the dark
in a park at nightfall.
Where the two of us would drift into the oblivion of a kiss.
And when there was a break in the rhythm,
I had your undivided attention.

We scheduled a rendezvous.
There in your home I felt as if I still knew you,
a nostalgia generated by the happiness
in pictures throughout the room,
in scenes I never knew.
Framed people in the two-faced confidence of youth
lacking the inclement weather
where we would argue,
pick holes in stone
smash bone with words,
and in that skip of tempo.
The illusion since removed.

Summer Dreams

I stare blatantly into the sun.
Pink hues of early morning undressed,
the nuance of a warm willingness
suppressed. When her face is overcast.
And late day in vivid twilight,
when the violet shade amazes
even the keenest eye.

She has two braids and shines in a dress,
mid-thigh high exposing the muscle line
that rarely elopes a panoply of peak interest.

The brevity is enormous;
it can be felt for ages.
In subterranean rooms
where she withers in my bloom,
it calls out to others
under the cover of night,
before the damp doings
of an Indian summer morning,
before the early warnings,
before the bragging rights.
Where pain is concealed in a fate
that doesn't exist on the existing plane
but in plain sight, so I abstain
from asking about anything permanent,
and lavish like a reptile in the sun.

It is Complicated

An employee required, formal affair.
Men dressed debonair and women brilliant in their jew-
elry.
The piano man taps at the black lacquered grand
atop the candelabra's flames, waver in and out
to the movement of the party and its sound.

You pass me in a large loop
like I am an extra on a movie shoot,
an unknown face off in the crowd.
Being lovely and loud, everyone notices you.
My eyes scurry across the floor.
In the limelight,
you stroll aloof and tightly aware of me.
But behind the scenes we share euphoric nights
where you deliberately
murmur so soft I have to lean in to hear.
Ours breaths coming so near I feel the tension,
I've never been so close to another spirit.
I can hear it in your voice too.
And as you career around exploiting men's need for con-
fidence,
I will never be the same again after this mess.
So I step outside and take the hurt
along with the fall in being the other guy.
I should have been a stunt double instead.

My First Taste of Immortality

Wind rasps within a plastic grocery sack
undulating for dear life on a naked tree branch.
Leaves roll above an abandoned street
in an unreal cadence.
I turn the spigot on, it reeks of rust,
then coughs and spits as words
linger on the tip of another's tongue.
And in a stray glimpse of coincidence
I feel closer to the other side,
like at the beginning of a memory that is ending.
As she says,
"I'm only into serious inquiries.
 I've got bigger fish to fry,
 and if I die, I die.
 But it won't be by my own hand."

In the immaterial world
the towering trees,
the inferno burns between the leaves,
then extends to the ground,
her breeze, swaying in the wind.
I'm hanging on
like a scrap of cloth
attached with a clothespin.
I could never comprehend
the simple things,
like her leaving me.
In hopes to contain
the impenetrable darkness,
I take stabs in the dark
at a different strain,

looking for a remedy.
I open a line of communication with the gods
to break the ice hidden between the stars.
As days carry on in a rabid bad habit,
and suffocate into nighttime,
inward grows this great expanse
that persists beyond known limits,
and shifts the temporal existence for good.

Fairy Tales of Youth

Peering into the lush quandary,
following you and your retinue,
while you squander the simple's dreams
with gestures laden in cosmetic trivialities.
Requisitioning poor souls,
dragging them through myriad toils
from pillow to pillow.
Asking if the gamble is worthwhile.
I lurch into the foray,
deploying an unorthodox snare,
a dubious air of authenticity,
in deft enquiries about your dreams,
as you talk about your favorite things.
In the continuous emergence of a delicate, slow smile,
I figure we'd be together for a while,
assuming I could deplete red flags by rubbing them pink.
Which over the years I was never able to do.
So I left you standing there,
staring at the last thing present in your mind,
before the expression of blank surprise,
before I rained on your parade.
And as you begin to fulminate on your take,
blaring retorts of pure disdain,
clips playing,
where you refrain from leaving me.
Bending to your cue, I would correct course,
ignoring the pending remorse in staying.
Reconciled by cries of the uncircumcised,
categorized in segments of sleepless fights,
those nights were the summit of our decline.
As I turn around to shout these things,

there you stand,
your makeup a facade of grace,
tears trailing down through the shortcomings of the
paint.
I hesitate and take a breather.
In the dark corners, in such a dark place,
where time had no face or value,
I left no promises to break.

Moving On

We bought a monster Cape Cod up north,
close to a beach on the far reaches of the city.
As I cover everything getting ready to head south alone,
I sit and watch the walls of a home brimming with
throws.
Like snow draping over the landscape,
thrown to cover the leftover mistakes,
hiding the specific details of a world.
Though if you try hard enough, you can recall
all the small things she left behind.
The surface drab and plain over the trailing waves
but teeming with life underneath – like a barrier reef.
Draping over a gaping hole in my heart that has no end
or start.
A rift so big it pulls my soul towards it,
renders me depleted
on the verge of defeated.
Temples – fingerprint indented from the strain
as my bones begin to splinter from the weight.
I grab my things and leave for good.
Only postponing the inevitable.

About a Girl

I look through a double plated window
at a suburb girl.
She works at Ross and she's
the pick of the litter.
And there, she has one too.
Her clothes are new – well, sort of.
She works at a register counting bills,
with little strands of hair
falling out of a messy bun,
gingerly lingering down her neck.
Perfume holds in the despair,
busy eyes,
scenarios of dread in her head,
hoping they won't come true, but if they do,
they'll haunt to death or as close as you'll ever come.
In between monetary miscues, she breaks,
fakes a smile or two for a minute.

I miss you - I thought you were going to say I do –
what the hell is your problem - why ain't I enough –
why am I never good enough - who knows if I'll make it
through –
how the hell will I make it without you!
Pondering how far away to run,
or maybe try and salvage this nightmare or, maybe
just move on.
Slowly and without one clue what happened to her.

The Clearing

Tell me it will be okay,
that these bodies
are only a temporary reprieve,
a stay, from the swirling.
Till we go back
to where we came
take another shape,
witness
the next set of stars
from a distance
so far we cannot imagine.

I give my two weeks' notice.
It's like
dragging the lake for dead bodies to finish.
So I can
let little parts of myself
out into the atmosphere,
where they'll choke on air
and find their meaning.

I assume at the appendix
the storylines will be fitting
and I believe there's a clearing,
where the cottonwood seeds drift edgewise
like awe at the first inset of snow.
Where my voice will not go unheard.

The words:
a mosaic painted
in flesh covered life,
(with a sliver of defiance)
which delves
into the inner workings
of the soul to see
what makes the heart sing
and at the crescendo,
used to ignite or divide us.

PART III: Ditto

The Cold Cuts

Some come for the cold cuts, they strut alongside their
wives,
whose tourniquet style strangles the blood-ties.
Some are more refined casually listening to some,
brooding over scandals, the prattling exacerbated by
wine.
Some bring white stargazers to perpetuate the charade,
placing them next to the raised bouquets on seats,
affixing them to the common theme,
a sundry meant to honor the grieving in process.

Shifting through debris of envy and praise.
I recede into the refuge of my breathing,
and ask without utterance,
was the transition from the temporal uneventful?
Certain things cannot be ascertained by abstract activity.
As the minister starts with his indoctrinated escapades.
I hear your voice amid my voice of reason,
far into the reaches of desiderium, then a few fathoms
deeper,
retracing steps close to nothingness,
it's blurry like a lucid dream, the shadows a bit sinister,
curling around a path to an upstairs window where
I see you posted at the sill poised.
Your brows concentrated into a frown,
knowing I would take the easy way out if you'd let me.
I feel your hands draw near and push me right through
the fear,
back into today where

I sense you here in times of need,
when needing you the most,
when I'm volatile and can't take anymore,
you jerk me up off the floor and I hear,
"Suck it up buttercup!"

Continuation

As you evacuate the body
through the lungs,
I breathe in your last gasp
of air and the fallout.
Then you are on a separate plane,
unavailable to me
even though I am also nowhere.

Sifting through the artifacts,
in the excavation of your home,
I come across your off-guard laugh
trapped in some photos
with splotches of sun spilled on them.
And marred in the assumption
that there was plenty of time
to do the things we liked,
to talk about over the phone.

I put one in my wallet,
take it out,
set the feelings free,
let the laughter fly
in cases of emergency.

You were the light,
flashing behind a keyhole
down a dark hall I could follow
to ask for some advice.
As I maneuver as best I can
away from the small straight
of a retained hallway.

You follow me in the idioms I say.
The words brush across my face,
a soft wind of remembering
once and again.
For I am landlocked
and you are free
to go wherever the trade winds roam
since I released you into the easterlies.

FNG

The new guy arrives in full battle dress,
we go over the tools to implement
for continued success in country
before his first patrol.

We are drenched in a shroud
of dense foliage and the stench of spoiling
flesh still fresh from yesterday's bayonet melee.
The point man tucks into a sudden rest
and pivots, his enormous eyes give warning
of the danger ahead, of the incoming, of the explosions
that upon impact jar souls loose from the skin.

Bullet holes clip the leaf tips, whip past ears,
the new guy over there is gurgling, his disappearance
will take years away from my sleep. I will see him later
rummaging through my nightmares,
a tenant of my dreams.

The new guy arrives in full battle dress,
we go over the tools to implement
for continued success in country
before his first patrol.

We requisition the hollows of a cave,
feet knee deep in muddy paste,
a tracer ricochets, strays on course.
As we shut his lids
it's like opening a cellar door and climbing in
as night descends and slips into the same dream,

into a sequence that never ends, only the tenants change.
The cost being paid solely at my expense.

Men are saran-wrapped in clear body bags.
Dog tags tied to their big toe exposed,
ready to be stowed for the lonely ride home.
I see their distorted faces.
The plastic clings to the elongated brows
stretching down along the eye sockets,
sucked in, suffocating at the mouth.

A Wish Unfolds

I'm here for some cognitive restructuring.
Please help me before I leap into the abyss.
I've tried doctors peddling their medication,
solutions so vague I drown in the excess.
They've given me your name and you're all that's left,
drawn to a dark summer sill accentuated by sunlight,
she politely asks me to sit, closes the shades and we be-
gin.

The convo is like an exorcism,
prizing those who refuse to concede,
into the light, so they can dissipate
in the exposure of ubiquitous insight.
Reliving scenarios over and over
until it gets deathly still,
building the tension to a climax,
where it's exhausting just to continue.

We do this for weeks upon end,
in attempts to partially patch the rifts,
although – they still thrive,
embedded in the neural beehive,
subdued but ready to rise, beyond plain view
targeting the chambers inside,
predominately at night,
incredulous eyes wide towards the catastrophic terrors
that comprise,
of the terse racket of the M60's,
rats and their slimy bellies
feeding on the over spray of grey.
From the bomb debris that blasted through and by.

A best friend while trying to tie a tourniquet,
these are where the flashbacks coincide
with the deep residual fractures of the mind,
and in the convalescence of a hospital bed
where the folding of a thousand origami cranes unfolds a
wish
and that wish is for death.

As suggested each day, I meditate
transferring into a prolonged theta state.
Now dreams are the only place I can't escape from them,
who were once my closest friends.
Thank you for the work done here.
Please forgive me if I interfered with your psyche.

Pondering Falls

I take a stroll down the street we used to live on,
where a few years prior I was looking out
a window that I'm spying in from the outside now,
not so far removed that I don't fall into a distant trance,
of watching the snow in the process of culminating on
the ground below.
The sky, faintly dark but grey as snow swoons over the
terrain,
drooping over daybreak, covering the depression, blan-
keting the obsession.

A Christmas tree in a shadowed corner, colorfully lit and
alternating red
and green.
Our relatives in their best Christmas attire,
tawdry sweaters that cause a little civil jest.
The spiked eggnog has a few sawing logs.
It seemed we would last the rest of our days content.
As I trowel the rough edges of our concrete animation,
I cannot figure out where the dire wrinkles existed,
and I can pick apart anything, pick flesh from bone, pick
holes in stone.

I took the Christmas tree down in your honor, waiting till
it withered,
like I was bartering with death, if it lived then maybe you
would come back.
Or perhaps,

I could exchange your life for mine, as if the tree had
some connection to the divine.
For then that would be that, instead of this filthy exis-
tence.

After the cremation was complete,
I walked the circumference of outside walls on rooftops,
looking down from ledges, pondering falls.
I didn't have the balls, my god you were brave!
Though you took the hurt and passed it on to the people
standing around your grave,
speaking in an undisclosed fashion,
reciting the whispers of a dead poet.
"With a sigh I resign, what I thought once was mine, and
forgive her deceit
with a tear."
The epitaph is clear.
I've no animosity towards you, dear. I just miss you,
right here, right now,
standing in front of what once was our house.

Before You Know It

Peeking past the curtains at the flower beds she made
grow,
with tedious transplanting in that first springtime,
when she decided to make it bloom – directly outside our
home.
The lilacs crisp – protruding from the ground,
from little dirt mounds at first,
then a thirst for life would reveal – the unwrinkled
flower,
with a few small showers to help – throughout a couple
intermittent days.
And here I stand staring out this window, prone
to memories laid so vividly open and bare,
where lilacs shone so candid you could touch them.
Your torso would pivot to catch my slow blinks,
the days so cute like a childhood crush,
never thinking to miss you much,
until you were a ghost emanating in the phrases I say.
Taking me back to being young and in love,
when with a brush of hair,
you interposed life over the landscape you chose.
And the paintings are the portraits hung about the house,
knitting our intricate existence together.
Along with your tidbits indented on the terrain,
along with your reproach – loud in my complaining,
interjecting your two cents, amplified by the strain.
Get off the couch and jump back into life or you'll join
me,
in the ground in the next grave.

The Ward

The manufactured breeze and cringes
when people sneeze can be felt for miles.
From an anonymous window,
the orange star hovers in the stare
from the smoke of forest fires
that highlight the atmosphere.
This is where emotions are held static
on the face for the sake of the failing.
The claustrophobia runs rampant
with personalities heaped on top of each other.
Some here, some there,
some have multiple to spare,
waiting in the wings,
dependent upon the hour,
which one decides,
to surface for air.

The desperation is
a tired you can never quite recover from.
The names are soon forgotten,
for only the first few were keepsakes.
And you can see the spread of fear
on the new faces,
like the terror of a child when night breaks.
When a widow comes
to commandeer the pieces of the deceased,
a to-do list, some car keys,
on the way to the morgue.

From the same window
dandelions are drab,
black and white
from lack of natural sunlight.
Frail, flimsy notes manifest
into a dose of humanness.
Trembling, the tumult shocks
like a sheet of glass that shatters on impact.
Severing that ounce of resistance
to give up and just go home.

The Last Step

We travel along this path of tears,
searching for perfect bodies,
you can see the travail in most of their eyes,
and you ignore it for fear of being lonely.
Love usually starts with trivialities,
shapes, flavor, sly grins from favors.
Who deciphers who is soulless.
Only you.
Oh, how early lovers love the nights,
wishing they could go on always.
Then the sun rushes in
and takes away the laughter.
Busy days cancel out those times,
as the end of fresh love begins,
with petty trivialities.

Two lonely people sit at a park bench,
try to think of what to say next,
when one says goodbye.
(It's never me, it's always them.)

There's a certain darkness
that cures in the night,
it's under my eyes and behind them,
all the way in, it festers to the soul.
No one wants to talk about it,
only the light,
no regrets left, no love, no life.
Ceiling fans spin endlessly across the world

in slow motion.
I tie a makeshift noose at the top of the stairs
and prepare to stare who knows where
but the already dead.
I stand on the threshold of dying in a panic.
The rope instantly snaps the fall.
Feet dangle above the top step swinging.
A cool draft creeps down the stairs and into the basement
along with a gust of despair.

ABOUT THE AUTHOR

The poetry collection, *A Record Of Change*, was an Amity Literary Prize finalist in 2023. Thaddeus Dugan resides in Topeka, Kansas and studies English/Writing at Washburn University. He has two cats, one named Araya and the other Eliot who supervise all his writing endeavors. In his spare time he likes to read, write and observe all the conditions of the human experience. Find him on Facebook as TA Dugan or Thaddeus A. Dugan, Author.

We hope you enjoyed reading Thaddeus A. Dugan's "A RECORD OF CHANGE." Please order additional print copies from https://anamcara-press.com/ or from your favorite bookseller and leave a review for Thaddeus on your favorite bookseller's website!

OTHER BOOKS TO ENJOY FROM ANAMCARA PRESS

ISBN: 9781941237-08-3
$14.99

ISBN: 9781941237-33-5
$18.99

ISBN: 9781941237-30-4
$18.99

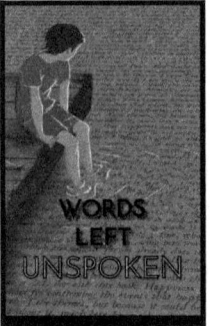

ISBN: 9781941237-13-7
$12.99

ISBN: 9781941237-18-2
29.99

ISBN: 9781941237-14-4
$14.99

Available wherever books are sold or at:
https://anamcara-press.com/

Thank you for being a reader! Anamcara Press publishes select works and brings writers & artists together in collaborations in order to serve community and the planet. *Your comments are always welcome!*

www.ingramcontent.com/pod-product-compliance
Lightning Source LLC
Chambersburg PA
CBHW070936120626
46546CB00004B/1434